# THE MEGA-FUN
# Multiplication Facts
# Activity Book

## Easy Games, Poems, Mini-Books, Reproducibles, and Memorization Strategies for Kids of All Learning Styles

### Marcia Miller & Martin Lee

SCHOLASTIC
PROFESSIONAL BOOKS

New York ❀ Toronto ❀ London ❀ Auckland ❀ Sydney

To Harpur and Calhoun, where it all started

Cover design by Vincent Ceci and Jaime Lucero

Cover art by Jo Lynn Alcorn

Interior illustrations by Ellen Joy Sasaki and Manuel Rivera

Interior design by Ellen Matlach Hassell
for Boultinghouse & Boultinghouse, Inc.

ISBN 0-590-37350-1

*Dear Teacher,*

*The more things change, the more they stay the same. Whatever your particular philosophy of education, experience, teaching style, class dynamics, or budget, you know you'll spend significant time helping students learn the basic multiplication facts. That's why this book is for you.*

The Mega-Fun Multiplication Facts Activity Book *is a storehouse of ideas on teaching, practicing, reinforcing, and applying the basic multiplication facts in ways students will enjoy. These classroom-tested activities are varied, easy to use, adaptable, and open-ended. They address students' different learning modalities. And they really work!*

*Happy teaching!*
Marcia Miller and Marty Lee

# Contents

## Big Ideas in Multiplication

## Setting the Tables

## Multiplication Applications and More!

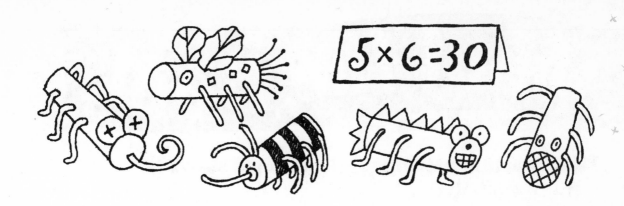

✳ Signifies reproducible page

## What is multiplication and when should students learn to multiply?

Simply put, multiplication is a special circumstance of addition in which all addends are the same size. Many childhood experiences use rudimentary multiplication: creating same-size groups for sharing, skip counting, or determining the number of slices of bread for family lunches. The right time to formally explore the concept of multiplication is whenever students have a grasp of counting, patterns, and conservation of number, and can work with numbers beyond 10. Memorizing multiplication facts is a skill most students achieve by third to fifth grade.

## Why teach the multiplication facts?

Children can multiply by counting or adding, but it's quicker to use the basic facts. Automaticity opens the door to other kinds of thinking. With the multiplication facts under their belts, students have a handy tool they can apply to the higher-level tasks of today's math curriculum.

## What are the best ways to approach multiplication?

Marilyn Burns discusses the importance of giving students adequate time to study and explore the meaning of an operation, such as multiplication, before concentrating on memorizing number facts. In *About Teaching Mathematics: A K–8 Resource*, she writes, "A premature focus gives weight to rote memorization, rather than keeping the emphasis on developing understanding of a new idea."

The most successful approach to multiplication is multifaceted: it combines counting; concrete experiences; mathematical communication; the use of models, manipulatives, and patterns; and the examination of multiplication situations from everyday life. Ideally, students learn number facts from repeated use in problem-solving and real-life situations. Games and other activities provide further practice and usually enhance recall once students have internalized the concepts.

## How can this book help?

This book is an anthology of activities, projects, and games designed to help students learn the basic multiplication facts. We believe that some drill and practice is required to help students memorize these facts. We hope our ideas will help make the process more appealing and exciting.

# Teaching Tips

This book is divided into three parts.

**BIG IDEAS IN MULTIPLICATION** gives generic ideas for exploring multiplication without regard to particular groups of facts or tables. Adapt the information here to fit your needs.

**SETTING THE TABLES** breaks down multiplication, fact by fact, starting with the zeros and moving through the twelves. Each group of ideas is targeted for a specific set of facts but can be adapted as needed.

**MULTIPLICATION APPLICATIONS AND MORE!** presents interactive bulletin board ideas, brief activities, puzzles, games, projects, and simulations to broaden the way you present multiplication in your classroom, plus handy reproducibles, a self-assessment log, and a literature list.

# Make It Work

- Go through the book in any order. Start anywhere and jump around. Revisit activities at any time during the year.

- Adapt activities presented for a particular set of facts to fit other facts. Or combine activities to provide mixed practice.

- You may find some activities too advanced for your class, while others are too basic. Revise or extend tasks to suit your needs.

- When you make manipulatives, such as factor cards, keep them for use in subsequent activities.

- Draw on students' prior knowledge and multiplication vocabulary. Encourage talking, questioning, sharing, recording, and summarizing.

- Notice the fact booklets in *Setting the Tables*. These hands-on study guides give students personalized aids for learning multiplication facts. Each fact booklet has a template students can trace and cut out to make their own booklets. The designs are simple, assembly is easy, and the result is invaluable and fun to use. If students make all the booklets, they'll have a full set of study guides.

- If possible, obtain the audiocassette *Times Tunes* by Marcia Miller (Scholastic, 1998), which presents twelve songs to help students learn the multiplication facts. Use the songs in harmony with activities from this book.

# Show It, Know It

The more students handle, manipulate, examine, and arrange objects, the more solidly they internalize the concepts the objects represent. Encourage students to make multiplication models as they explore the concept of multiplication and learn the products of multiplication facts. Here are some ideas.

## Beans!

Have students glue dried beans onto oak tag to form multiplication arrays. They count the beans to form the arrays and they touch them for a tactile review of the value of the array. And the beans look great on display!

## Straw Bundles

Have students tape or tie together sets of drinking straws to model equal-group representations of multiplication facts.

## Loops and Groups

Children can use pieces of yarn to form loops. Each loop will represent a set. Have students place the same number of objects within each loop to represent a multiplication situation. For example, a student can make 4 loops of yarn and put 5 teddy bear counters in each to show that $4 \times 5 = 20$.

## Strings and Things

In this variation on Loops and Groups, students use string to section off parts of the tabletop or work area. In each section, they put equal numbers of objects. They write a multiplication number sentence for the model.

## Crisscross Products

Children can use plain paper to show multiplication facts. For instance, to show $6 \times 4$, they draw 6 horizontal lines on paper. Then they draw 4 vertical lines across the horizontal ones and make an × or dot on each intersection. This resembles the array model of multiplication and provides students with a tool they can use to figure out any product, even if they have no special math materials on hand.

## Bracelets

Have students make simple bracelets of equal numbers of beads or macaroni. They can wear the bracelets for a day as they try to memorize a fact. For example, to learn $4 \times 9 = 36$, they wear four 9-bead bracelets, which they can count and recount as necessary to learn the fact.

# Big Ideas in Multiplication

## Groups vs. Arrays

Initial presentations of multiplication usually show repeated groups of the same size. Preliminary multiplication experiences should provide students with many opportunities to form same-size groups and count the total, or product. Easy-to-obtain materials for such explorations include paper cups and crayons, egg cartons and dried beans, yarn and beads, coins and change purses, or any other objects that can be easily grouped and counted by sets.

It would be incomplete to model multiplication only as sets of separate, same-size groups. Another important multiplication model is the *array*. An array is a rectangular arrangement in rows and columns. The array model appears most often when multiplication is used to explore area measure. But the array model is a valid one students should investigate. Arrays are easy to arrange and can be pleasing to the eye.

Grid paper is a readily available material students can use to explore arrays. With grid paper, they can make borders around arrays of various dimensions. They can cut out arrays and label them with the facts that fit. They can rotate arrays to grasp the order (commutative) property of multiplication: $3 \times 4 = 4 \times 3$.

Other materials students can use to make array models include snap cubes, Cuisenaire rods, color tiles, carpet squares, seating charts, sheets of stamps or stickers, and calendars.

To assess their understanding of multiplication, have students draw or model a multiplication fact as a set of equal groups, such as 4 paws on each of 3 kittens for 12 paws in all, as well as an array, such as 4 columns of 3 boxes in each column.

4 paws x 3 kittens = 12 paws

4 x 3 = 12

# Properties of Multiplication

Multiplication has certain rules students will discover as they begin to understand the operation. These *properties* also serve as thinking strategies students can apply to problem-solving situations.

**COMMUTATIVE PROPERTY** Like addition, multiplication is commutative: the *order* of factors does not change the product. Knowing this property can become a key idea students can use to take charge of their learning. Have them make models to demonstrate and prove that $7 \times 3$ has the same product as $3 \times 7$.

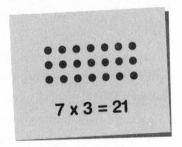

7 x 3 = 21

3 x 7 = 21

**ASSOCIATIVE PROPERTY** This rule states that no matter how you *group* factors, the product will be the same: $(a \times b) \times c = a \times (b \times c)$. Children can grasp this idea by relating it to column addition, in which they can group addends in any convenient way to find the sum. Similarly, students can group factors in any way that works best as they seek the product. Some students may see this rule as an extension of the commutative property of multiplication.

**IDENTITY PROPERTY** Children usually learn this property as the "1 rule" for multiplication. Simply put, the product of any number and 1 is that number itself. Encourage students to find examples of this property in the classroom. For instance, one group of 4 desks is 4 desks. One row on the calendar, which shows 7 days, is 7. Children may enjoy extending this rule to the absurd: $1 \times$ a gazillion = 1 gazillion, or $1 \times$ a kumquat = 1 kumquat.

**ZERO PROPERTY** In addition, adding zero to a number does not change its identity: $n + 0 = n$. But in multiplication, any number multiplied by zero is zero: $n \times 0 = 0$. Again, encourage students to find examples of this property in the classroom. For instance, in a classroom that has 28 desks and 0 elephants sitting on each, there are 0 elephants in all. The absurd is equally entertaining with zero: $0 \times 88$ billion = 0, $0 \times$ tuna fish = 0, and so on.

**DISTRIBUTIVE PROPERTY OF MULTIPLICATION OVER ADDITION** This rule, symbolized as $a(b + c) = (ab) + (ac)$ "distributes," or spreads out, the value of *a* equally to both *b* and to *c*. Children apply this rule intuitively as they solve harder multiplication facts. For instance, for $6 \times 7$, they might think: $(6 \times 6) + (6 \times 1)$, or $36 + 6 = 42$. Children can model and explore this property with arrays, grid paper, or cups and beans.

# Tried-and-True Times Techniques

**Here are some approaches you can use with any set of multiplication facts. Mix and match as you want to create mixed practice.**

**SKIP COUNTING** Encourage students to use skip counting at any opportunity: to count milk money, take attendance, count out art supplies, and so on. Most students can count by 2s, 5s, and 10s. You can help them learn to count by 3s or by any other number.

**BUZZ!** This old game still works and requires no materials at all! Identify the "buzz" number, such as all multiples of 7. Children begin to count off, one number at a time. Whoever should say a multiple of 7, such as 7 or 14, says "Buzz!" instead. The count-off continues until students reach a target number, such as 100, or until they all foul out. For more advanced students, try playing Zzub! In this variation of the game, start at a higher number, such as 72, and count back toward zero. Again, identify the Zzub number before you start.

**MINI-TABLES** To focus on the facts in a particular table, students can make strip charts, fact wheels, or flip books. First they can make these in times table order as they start to learn the facts. Later, they can make fact wheels or flip books that give facts in mixed order for a greater challenge.

**WALK-ON NUMBER LINES** Make a walk-on number line in your classroom by putting masking tape on the floor and numbering it. Or use a plastic shower curtain or painter's drop cloth and paint a number line on it. Have students practice skip counting by walking along the number line and stepping on (or avoiding) the multiples of a given number.

**CALCULATOR CONSTANTS** If your classroom calculators have a constant function, students can use them to investigate the multiples of any number and to make the link between addition and multiplication. Here's what to do:

◉ Select a factor, such as 6. Enter it.

◉ Press the + key, then press the = key. The display should show 6 again.

◉ Now, keep pressing the = key. The constant function will add 6 over and over; the display will show the multiples of 6.

The constant function will work as long as students keep pressing the = key. They can go as high as they wish. Have students record the multiples and look for patterns in their list.

**SONGS** Music and rhythm are great ways for students to learn and memorize ideas. Obtain a copy of *Times Tunes* by Marcia Miller and play it as time permits. Or encourage the musical/rhythmic learners in your class to make up multiplication chants, raps, or tunes they can share with classmates.

# Build and Use Fact Tables

Most experts agree that students should not work to fill in an entire multiplication fact table until they have a firm grasp on the concept of multiplication, understand the meaning of an array, know how to read a table in rows and columns, and know some basic facts. But once students reach this point, there are many productive ways they can use a multiplication fact table. Here are some ideas.

## Square Numbers

Explore with students the meaning of square numbers. Have them use color tiles or paper squares to model square numbers. Then have them identify and fill in the products of square numbers on the multiplication chart and describe the patterns they see.

## Easy Ones First

To many students, completing an entire blank table seems like an enormous and daunting assignment. Simplify the process by encouraging students to fill in the "easy ones" first. For instance, students can easily fill in the rows and columns for the zeros and 1s, maybe also for the 2s, 5s, and 10s. When these products are in place, help students see that there are fewer empty boxes—and not so many more facts to learn.

## Facts Focus

Use crepe paper streamers or shelf paper edging to highlight and outline a particular row or column of the multiplication chart. Explain that these are the featured facts to focus on today. Have students fill in the facts for that row or column and refer to it throughout the day.

See the activities on page 50 for more ideas.

| ×  | 0 | 1  | 2  | 3  | 4  | 5  | 6  | 7  | 8  | 9  | 10  |
|----|---|----|----|----|----|----|----|----|----|----|-----|
| 0  | 0 | 0  | 0  | 0  | 0  | 0  | 0  | 0  | 0  | 0  | 0   |
| 1  | 0 | 1  | 2  | 3  | 4  | 5  | 6  | 7  | 8  | 9  | 10  |
| 2  | 0 | 2  | 4  | 6  | 8  | 10 | 12 | 14 | 16 | 18 | 20  |
| 3  | 0 | 3  | 6  | 9  | 12 | 15 | 18 | 21 | 24 | 27 | 30  |
| 4  | 0 | 4  | 8  | 12 | 16 | 20 | 24 | 28 | 32 | 36 | 40  |
| 5  | 0 | 5  | 10 | 15 | 20 | 25 | 30 | 35 | 40 | 45 | 50  |
| 6  | 0 | 6  | 12 | 18 | 24 | 30 | 36 | 42 | 48 | 54 | 60  |
| 7  | 0 | 7  | 14 | 21 | 28 | 35 | 42 | 49 | 56 | 63 | 70  |
| 8  | 0 | 8  | 16 | 24 | 32 | 40 | 48 | 56 | 64 | 72 | 80  |
| 9  | 0 | 9  | 18 | 27 | 36 | 45 | 54 | 63 | 72 | 81 | 90  |
| 10 | 0 | 10 | 20 | 30 | 40 | 50 | 60 | 70 | 80 | 90 | 100 |

# Why Memorize?

Children often ask why they should learn multiplication facts by heart. Discuss the idea that while it's important to understand the meaning behind the facts and it's terrific to know how to figure them out, mathematicians prefer to spend their energy on more challenging, puzzling ideas. Explain that the key job of mathematics is to apply what you know to solve problems—that's what takes the most brain power. Emphasize that by committing the facts to memory, the brain is free to concentrate on harder, more interesting, or more valuable tasks.

Brainstorm a list of some of the things students know by heart: Mom's birthday, an old nursery rhyme, a best friend's phone number, the recipe for French toast. Although some of these things are actually much more complex to recall than number facts, most people know them by heart.

Post this poem on the chalkboard or read it to the class. Talk about its meaning.

## It's Wise to Memorize

The teacher asks for four times eight, you wonder what to do.
You model and draw and count and add to get to thirty-two.
Yes, it's thirty-two, but if I were you I'd want a faster way,
So learn by heart the product part to have more time to play.

    What you know by heart sets you apart,
    It's wise to memorize,
    So use your brain to make it plain,
    It's wise to memorize.

When a problem asks for eight times six, you can worry, you can fret.
Add sixes until you've done all eight. What number will you get?
Yes, it's forty-eight, but what a wait as you calculate away!
So learn by heart the product part to have more time to play.

    What you know by heart sets you apart,
    It's wise to memorize,
    So use your brain to make it plain,
    It's wise to memorize.

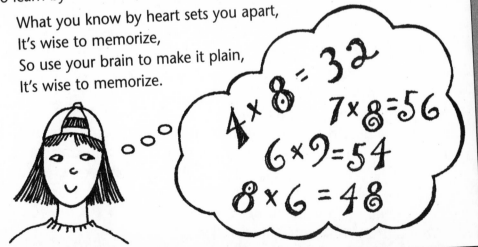

$$4 \times 8 = 32$$
$$7 \times 8 = 56$$
$$6 \times 9 = 54$$
$$8 \times 6 = 48$$

# Setting the Tables

## 0 AS A FACTOR

**Multiplying by zero can be a strange concept for some students to grasp. Spend time helping students visualize zero groups of *n*, or groups of *n* zero times.**

### STORY
### Lots of No Mail

This story helps students grasp why any number times zero is zero. Read this story to the class, post it on chart paper to read together, use it as a Readers' Theater skit with different students taking each role, or record it so students can listen to it independently. Invite them to act out the story. Discuss the pattern, the logic, the humor, and the generalizations about multiplying by zero that they can make. You can provide the equations that represent each person's "zero pieces of mail" or derive them with the class as you read.

Neighbors in an apartment house met at the mailboxes each day at 2:00 P.M. to get the mail. They loved getting mail. They loved meeting at the same time each day to chat. And they all loved sharing the best mail with each other.

One Monday, Rex opened his mailbox. "Oh!" he cried. "It's empty! I got zero pieces of mail. There are no letters in here. Can you believe it? Zero!" *(1 x 0 = 0)*

"Bummer," said Juan. Then he opened his mailbox. "Hey!" he cried. "I got no letters. *And* I got no postcards. I got more nothing than Rex did!" *(2 x 0 = 0)*

Katy opened her mailbox. Her smile faded. "Zero mail for me, too. I got no letters, no postcards, *and* no magazines. That's even more no mail!" *(3 x 0 = 0)*

"It's a bad mail day for me, too," said Tia. "I got even more nothing than Katy. I got no letters, no postcards, no magazines, *and* no catalogs." *(4 x 0 = 0)*

"This is weird," said Marnie. "I got even more nothing than Tia, because I got no letters, no postcards, no magazines, no catalogs, *and* no bills." *(5 x 0 = 0)*

"You think that's bad?" Jill whined. "I got the most nothing so far! I got no letters, no postcards, no magazines, no catalogs, no bills, *and* no store flyers." *(6 x 0 = 0)*

"Yeah, yeah," said Zeke. "I got the most nothing. I got no letters, no postcards, no magazines, no catalogs, no bills, no store flyers, *and* no junk mail!" *(7 x 0 = 0)*

Tears came to Fred's eyes as he opened his mailbox. "Aw, even more nothing! I got no letters, no postcards, no magazines, no catalogs, no bills, no store flyers, no junk mail, *and*..." he sniffed, "...no birthday cards." *(8 x 0 = 0)*

"Your birthday isn't until Thursday," said Katy.

"So?" Fred whimpered, "somebody could send me an early card."

"Sorry, Fred," said Corinne. "Now I'll look." She held her breath and peeked inside. "This is rotten," she said. "More nothing! I got no letters, no postcards, no magazines, no catalogs, no bills, no store flyers, no junk mail, no birthday cards, *and* no packages." *(9 x 0 = 0)*

"Well, friends," announced Kim, "I have the most nothing of all. My zero mail is more zero mail than anyone else's. I got no letters, no postcards, no magazines, no catalogs, no bills, no store flyers, no junk mail, no birthday cards, no packages, *and* I got no E-mail!" *(10 x 0 = 0)*

◉ Who got the most nothing? What does that mean?

◉ What multiplication rule does the story prove?

## MODEL
# Zero Groups

Have students make up situations that yield a product of zero. The more creative and far-fetched, the better! For example, ask two volunteers to stand. Say, "I see two students. I see zero beards on each face. How many beards in all?" Guide students to respond, "Zero, because two times zero is still zero."

Children can work in small groups or as a whole class to invent and model situations about something zero times, or zero times something. You might compile examples in a class booklet or on chart paper.

## TRICK
# Amazing Speed Multiplying

Present the following seemingly difficult multiplication problems to students. Challenge them to find the products any way they can. Allow them to use calculators if they want. Then say that clever mathematicians can solve any of these problems in less than one second. How? What's the trick? *(Any number times zero is zero, no matter how great the number and no matter how many factors you multiply.)* Invite students to make up their own "impossibly hard" trick multiplication problems for classmates and family members to solve.

◉ 1 x 2 x 3 x 4 x 5 x 6 x 7 x 8 x 9 x 0 = ? *(0)*

◉ 865 million x 0 = ? *(0)*

◉ 12,345 x 6,789 x 0 = ? *(0)*

## SONG
# "I've Got Plenty o' Nothin'"

Play the song "I've Got Plenty o' Nothin'," from *Porgy and Bess* by George Gershwin. Go over the lyrics with students. Help them understand the idea that no matter how much nothing you have, it's still nothing, and sometimes a lot of nothing can be better than some (or lots!) of something you don't want.

# 1 AS A FACTOR

The factors of 1 are the same as the counting numbers. Children can multiply by 1 simply by understanding that something one time means the same as *just once*. So 1 dozen eggs is 1 set of 12, or 1 x 12, or 12.

## CHANT
# Here's the 1s

Use this poem as a rhythmic chant or present it for choral reading. Invite musical learners to create a tune or rhythmic accompaniment for the lyrics. Talk about what the words mean. You might perform this chant for other classes.

One times any number is that number,
One times one is one, that's clear to see.
One times two is two, and one times three is simply three,
Do the ones once more, I say, *encore*!
Let's do them, one, two, three!

    Here's the ones, ones, ones,
    The facts are so much fun.
    The ones you can't forget,
    The ones you know, I bet.
    Here's the ones, ones, ones
    Products roll off your tongues,
    It's the ones, you can multiply by one!

One times four is four, you know, I tell you it's no trick,
One times five is five, I say, and one times six is six.
One times seven is seven, and I bet you know the rest,
Do the ones once more, I say, *encore*!
Let's do them, they're the best!

    Here's the ones...

One times eight is eight, you see, and one times nine is nine,
One times ten is ten, my friends, and now you're gonna shine!
No matter what the factor that you multiply by one,
Do the ones once more, I say, *encore*!
You know them, everyone!

    Here's the ones...

# TRICK
# Fantastic Factors!

Children enjoy big numbers. And they love the being able to take charge of big numbers and operate on them. Like the Amazing Speed Multiplying trick students use when they multiply by 0, the multiplying by 1 rule lends itself to Fantastic Factors. Present these and others like them with high drama; greet the products with suitable amazement.

- ◎ 1 x 47 = ? *(47)*
- ◎ 1 x 239 = ? *(239)*
- ◎ 1 x 367,518 = ? *(367,518)*
- ◎ 1 x 16 million = ? *(16 million)*
- ◎ 1 x 99 billion = ? *(99 billion)*
- ◎ frog x 1 = ? *(frog)*
- ◎ hippopotamus x 1 = ? *(hippopotamus)*
- ◎ super-large french fries x 1 = ? *(super-large french fries)*

# CONCEPT
# Identity

In formal mathematical terms, multiplying by 1 reveals the *identity* property of multiplication. Simply put, the product of any number and 1 is that number itself. Multiplying by 1 produces the *identity* of the other factor.

Apply this concept to play Find the Factor. Pretend you are a detective. You know a secret factor, which you write on a slip or paper or index card. Do not show this to the class. Then say, "Only I know the identity of a secret factor. To find out what number it is, I will answer one and only one question. If you ask the right question, you'll always learn the identity of my secret factor."

Some students may make wild guesses, such as, "Is it 5? Is it 23?" Allow time for students to try to figure out the key question to ask. Guide them by giving this hint: "Ask me what the product is if I multiply my number by 1." Have a volunteer ask you that question. Give the truthful answer and reveal the number you wrote down. Help students realize that multiplying by 1 gives the identity of the secret factor.

Invite students to play in small groups, or have volunteers act as the detective. Clever detectives can try to trick classmates by using 0, 1, a fraction, or a money amount as the secret factor. But the identity rule of multiplication always works.

# 2 AS A FACTOR

Doubles, twins, partners—most students have had many informal experiences multiplying by 2. The 2s are among the easiest multiplication facts for most students to learn.

## FACT BOOKLET
## Butterfly 2s

Use the pattern below as a template for an individual fact booklet for the 2s. Discuss why a butterfly is an appropriate shape to use for a booklet about 2s. *(Butterflies have 2 wings.)* Have students trace and cut out 11 copies of the shape from white or colored paper. On each butterfly shape, have them write a 2 fact and its product, from $0 \times 2 = 0$ through $10 \times 2 = 20$. Help them attach the pages in order with yarn, a paper fastener, or staples. Children can customize each page with an icon, a design, or a special color that can help them recall the facts. Children can use the booklets to study the 2s on their own.

## BRAINSTORM
# Two by Two

Work with the whole class or form small groups. First, challenge students to brainstorm things that always come in a set of two, such as eyes, ears, mittens, socks, and so on. Allow about ten minutes for students to think. Next, compile a group list on chart paper or on the chalkboard. Then use the list to create funny story problems. For instance:

⊚ Three nearsighted giraffes wear contact lenses. How many contact lenses in all? *(6)*

⊚ Five polar bears wear earmuffs. How many ears are covered? *(10)*

## MANIPULATIVES
# Mirror Doubles

Help students realize that multiplying by 2 is like adding doubles. A concrete way to reinforce this idea is by using a mirror and any manipulative objects you have at hand: counters, blocks, crayons, straws, and so on. Have students make a group of some number of objects. Then have them hold a mirror near the group and write a multiplication number sentence to match what they see in all. Suppose a student makes a group of 7 straws. When the mirror is held near the group, 2 groups of 7, or 14 straws will be visible: the 7 actual straws and the 7 images in the mirror. The multiplication equation is $2 \times 7 = 14$.

## MODEL
# Neat Feet Floor Mat

Help students create a floor mat that shows pairs of footprints. Use a plastic shower curtain, tape, and contact paper. Tape a line across the shower curtain. Help students trace their feet on the contact paper, then cut out the shapes. Peel off the backing and stick on the pair of feet so that one foot of each pair falls on either side of the line. Tape the mat to the floor. Invite students to step on the footprints as they practice the 2s.

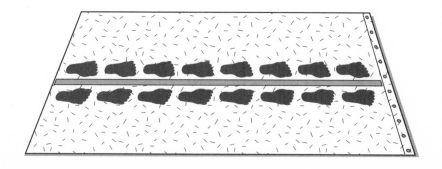

# PHYSICAL ACTIVITY
# Kangaroo Count-Off

Talk with students about how kangaroos hop. They keep both back legs together and push off with their tails. Invite students to practice kangaroo hops outside on the playground, or indoors in the gym or along a corridor. Guide students to notice that each time they jump they make a pair of footprints. If they jumped in paint or in snow, they could see their footprints.

As students jump, have them count off by twos: 2, 4, 6, 8, and so on. You might have various contests based on kangaroo hops. For instance:

- Whose 4 x 2 hops cover the greatest distance?

- How few hops can a person make between points *A* and *B?* What multiplication equation represents the number of hops?

- How many hops can you make without losing count as you skip-count by 2s?

# VOCABULARY
# Terms of 2

Work with the class to create a list of words, phrases, or expressions that suggest 2s or doubles. Examples include *twins, pair, partners, duo, couple, twosome, copycat,* and *like two peas in a pod.* Invite students to illustrate each word, phrase, or expression and compile a class booklet of *2 Terms.*

# 3 AS A FACTOR

Trios, triplets, three-packs—most students have seen many real-world objects that customarily come in sets of three. The 3s are relatively easy for most students to learn, and many students can learn to skip-count by 3s.

## FACT BOOKLET
## Triangle 3s

Use the pattern below as a template for an individual fact booklet for the 3s. Discuss why a triangle is a suitable shape to use for a booklet about 3s. *(Triangles have 3 sides and 3 angles.)* Have students trace and cut out 11 copies of the shape from white or colored paper. On each shape, have them write a 3 fact and its product, from $0 \times 3 = 0$ through $10 \times 3 = 30$. Help them attach the pages in order with yarn, a paper fastener, or staples. Children may customize each page with a symbol, a design, or a special color that can help them recall the facts. Children can use the booklet to study the 3s on their own.

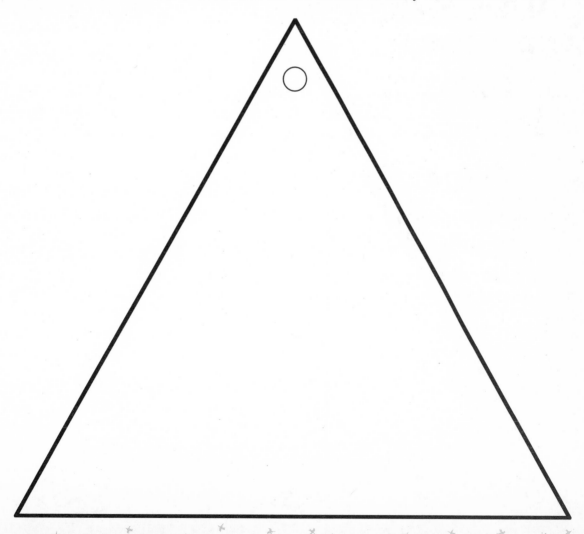

## ART
# Juice-Box Apartments

Many individual servings of fruit juice come in small boxes, which are frequently sold in packs of three. Ask students to collect empty juice boxes. Remind students to rinse them out with warm, soapy water to avoid bad smells and unwanted pests. Guide students to use the boxes to make "apartment buildings" that are 3 boxes wide or 3 boxes tall. Help them tape boxes together. Children can cover the boxes with contact paper, construction paper, or wallpaper scraps. Or add a few drops of liquid detergent to tempera paint so students can paint right onto the boxes. Assemble a juice-box neighborhood. When students determine an arrangement of the "apartment buildings," give each building a mailbox with a house number that is a multiple of three: 3, 6, 9, 12, 15, and so on. Children can "mail" slips of paper with multiplication facts in the 3s to the apartment house whose "address" matches the product on the slip.

## PHYSICAL ACTIVITY
# Triple Jump

Combine movement with learning the products of 3. Explain to students the Olympic event called the triple jump (once known as the hop, step, and jump). Ask a volunteer to demonstrate the event: The athlete takes a running start. On reaching the takeoff line, the person *hops* off on one foot, then *steps* onto the other foot, then *jumps* to a two-footed landing. The triple jump is measured by total distance from take-off line to landing point. No stopping or extra steps are permitted between the parts of the event.

Have students form triple jump teams of ten. Children will count as they do the triple jump but verbalize only the number they say on the two-footed landing: "(1, 2) **3**." Team members take turns jumping so that each student does one triple jump but the whole group counts off together to 30. When the second jumper goes, the group counts "(4, 5) **6**"; for the third jumper it's "(7, 8), **9**," and so on. You might measure and compare the distances jumped, or have groups practice synchronizing jumps, like a precision athletics team.

# 4 AS A FACTOR

Quartets, quadrupeds, and quadruplets—many kinds of foursomes exist in the worlds of music, science, and technology. Learning the 4s will proceed smoothly for students who know the 2s and grasp the concept of doubling.

## FACT BOOKLET
## Four-Leaf Clover 4s

Use the pattern below as a template for an individual fact booklet for the 4s. Discuss why this kind of clover is a good shape to use for a booklet about 4s. *(It has 4 leaves.)* Have students trace and cut out 11 copies of the clover shape from white or colored paper. On each clover, have them write a 4 fact and its product, from $0 \times 4 = 0$ through $10 \times 4 = 40$. Help them attach the pages in order with yarn, a paper fastener, or staples. Children may customize each page with a symbol or a special design that can help them recall the facts. Children can use the booklet to study the 4s on their own.

## ART
# Paper Chains

Children can make paper chains to help them visualize groups of 4. Prepare strips of colored paper students can use to form interlocking loops. They can use tape, paste, or staples to attach the ends of the loops. Encourage students to create a pattern in which each fourth loop stands out. For instance, they might do red, red, red, blue...; or three different colors, then white...; or hang a loop from the fourth loop to hold the entire number sentence. Hang the paper chains around the room so students can look for products as they practice the 4s.

## POEM
# Facts of 4

Post the chorus for a poem shown at right on the chalkboard or on chart paper.

Invite students to add original verses to the poem until it includes all the facts of 4. They may use any rhyme scheme, as long they maintain the rhythm of the poem. For instance, a student might write about $4 \times 4 = 16$ like this:

> One, two, three, four,
> Make a square and slam the door.
> Side by side and wall by floor,
> Find the facts of four.

> Four cars drive a bumpy road,
> Each tire hits some rocks,
> Four poor cars have four flat tires,
> That's sixteen bumpy shocks!

Post the poem. Have volunteers read verses aloud, or hold a choral reading.

## CONCEPT
# Doubling Doubles

Help students discover the relationship between the 2s and the 4s. Challenge students to show how, say, $4 \times 6$ is the same as $(2 \times 6) + (2 \times 6)$. Tell students to make 4 groups of 6 with snap cubes, counters, or other objects. Guide them to rearrange the 4 groups of 6 into 2 sets of $2 \times 6$. Model how to record the product as a series of additions of doubles. This technique won't save time for quick recall, but it provides a solid conceptual basis students can rely on to recall a fact in the 4s.

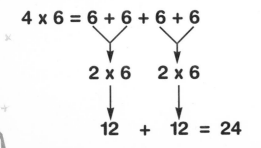

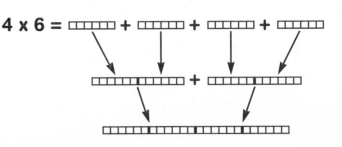

# 5 AS A FACTOR

Quintets, nickels, fingers, basketball teams—many kinds of 5s appear in the realm of money, time, counting, and sports. Because 5s are so prevalent in our base-10 numeration system, most students learn them quickly.

## FACT BOOKLET
## Star 5s

Use the pattern below as a template for an individual fact booklet for the 5s. Discuss why this kind of star is a good shape to use for a booklet about 5s. *(It has 5 points.)* Have students trace and cut out 11 copies of the star shape from white or colored paper. On each star, have them write a 5 fact and its product, from $0 \times 5 = 0$ through $10 \times 5 = 50$. Help them attach the pages in order with yarn, a paper fastener, or staples. Children may customize each page with a symbol, a color, or small stick-on stars that can help them recall the facts. Children can use the booklet to study the 5s on their own.

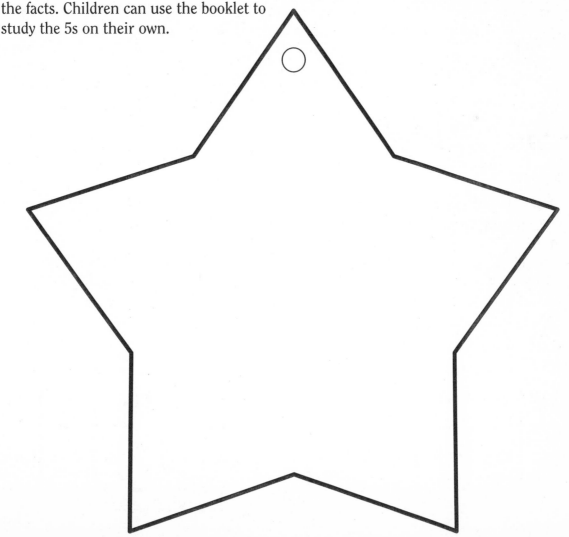

1 x 5 = 5 fingers or 1 handprint

2 x 5 = 10 fingers or 2 handprints

3 x 5 = 15 fingers or 3 handprints

## ART
# Show of Hands!

Help students create a mural of handprints to reinforce their learning of the facts of 5. Post a large piece of butcher paper on a wall, door, or bulletin board. Prepare some finger paint or tempera paint into which students can dip their hands to make contact prints on the paper. Or provide markers students can use to outline their hands on the mural paper. Have students group their hand prints to represent the 5 facts: $1 \times 5 = 1$ handprint or 5 fingers, $2 \times 5 = 2$ hand prints or 10 fingers, and so on. Invite volunteers to write a number fact for each group of handprints so that the mural is instructive as well as colorful.

## MANIPULATIVES
# Nickels

Children love to count money. Most have already had experience counting by 5s because they have counted nickels. Obtain a quantity of real or play nickels. Have students count by 5s as they count out varying amounts of nickels up to 10 nickels (50 cents). They might play a game with nickels to see who can accumulate money the fastest. Students can pick a number card from 0 to 10, take that many nickels, tell how much money they have, and keep a running total of their money as they practice the 5s.

If you have access to money stamps or stickers, students can use them to make a "nickels ribbon" to use to practice counting by 5s.

| 0 5¢ | 1 5¢ | 2 5¢ | 3 5¢ | 4 5¢ | 5 5¢ | 6 5¢ | 7 5¢ | 8 5¢ | 9 5¢ | 10 5¢ |
|---|---|---|---|---|---|---|---|---|---|---|
| 0 | 5¢ | 10¢ | 15¢ | 20¢ | 25¢ | 30¢ | 35¢ | 40¢ | 45¢ | 50¢ |

# MODEL
## Clockface 5s

Display an analog clock that's calibrated to the minute and that has the numbers 1–12. Review how to tell time on this kind of clock. Be sure students understand the meaning of the small tick marks *(minutes)* and the number of minutes that each large numeral represents. *(5)* Practice counting by 5s as a volunteer points to the corresponding numeral on the clock or moves the minute hand around the clockface. Help students make the connection between counting by 5s and knowing the products of the 5s as they appear on the clockface. That is, 1:40 means 40 minutes after 1. However, there is no 40 on the clock face, so we learn to count by 5s until we reach 40, which is at the 8; so, $8 \times 5 = 40$. Encourage students to look at the classroom clock to help them remember their fives.

# PATTERN
## Multiples of 5

Write the products of the 5s in a row across the board, or highlight that row on a multiplication chart. Ask students to look for patterns in the products. Most will notice that all products of 5 end either in 0 or 5, and that the ending numbers alternate. Guide students to generalize about all products of 5, even those far beyond the scope of the table. Then challenge them to figure out which ones end in 0 and which end in 5. *(Products of even numbers and 5 end in 0; products of odd numbers and 5 end in 5.)* Extend their understanding by asking whether the product of, say, $371 \times 5$ will end in 0 or in 5 and why. *(It ends in 5 because 371 is an odd number.)* Try again with other examples, such as $88 \times 5$ or $50,000 \times 5$. *(Both end in 0 because each non-5 factor is an even number.)*

| 0 | 5 | 10 | 15 | 20 | 25 | 30 | 35 | 40 | 45 | 50 |

# 6 AS A FACTOR

Six-packs of soda, insect legs, English muffins—sixsomes appear frequently in the real lives of students. Because the products grow larger, the 6s may be tricky for some students. Try a varied approach to help them make sense of the 6s.

## FACT BOOKLET
## Hexagon 6s

Use the pattern below as a template for an individual fact booklet for the 6s. Discuss why this geometric shape suits a booklet about 6s. *(Hexagons have 6 sides and 6 angles.)* Have students trace and cut out 11 copies of the hexagon from white or colored paper. On each one, have them write a 6 fact and its product, from $0 \times 6 = 0$ through $10 \times 6 = 60$. Help them attach the pages in order with yarn, a paper fastener, or staples. Children may customize each page with an icon, a symbol, a color, or a pattern that can help them recall the facts. Children can use the booklet to study the 6s on their own.

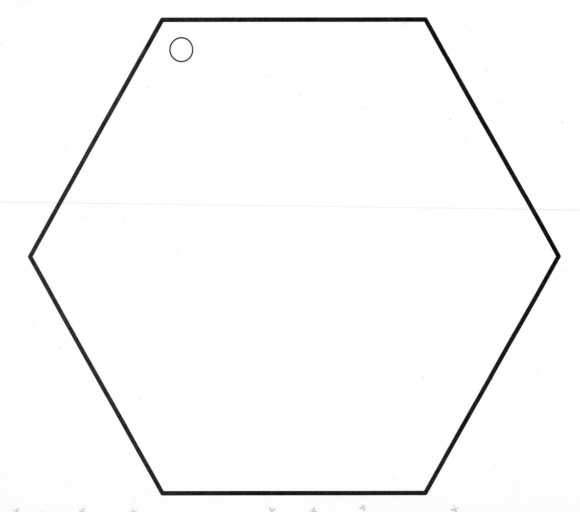

## SCIENCE
# Insects on Parade

Because the products of the 6s grow quite large, it helps students develop a sense for their relative magnitude to see the facts represented in models. Use a study of insects as a takeoff point for the 6s. Have students collect empty cardboard tubes from toilet tissue, wrapping paper, or paper towels. Use a razor blade knife to cut the tubes into lengths of about 4 to 4½ inches to serve as insect bodies. Provide pipe cleaners students can use to form legs—6 per insect, 3 on a side. They can use scraps of tissue paper, construction paper, foil, or fabric to decorate the insects as they wish. They can model their insects after real ones or make them fanciful. Set up a parade of insects walking in groups of 0, 1, 2, 3, and so on, through 10. (This takes 55 models.) Have students make a sign for each group of insects with the multiplication fact for the total number of legs in that group, such as $3 \times 6 = 18$.

## ECOLOGY
# 6-Pack Rings

Have students collect the plastic rings used to hold 6-packs of beverage cans. Cover a bulletin board with dark paper. Use the rings as array models of groups of 6. Tack the rings onto the board so they're easy to see. Have students label the arrays. Leave the display of 6-pack rings up as students learn the 6 facts.

Talk with students about the harm plastic 6-pack rings can bring to wildlife. Explain that people who litter the rings create traps for animals. Fishing birds can get them wrapped around their necks or tangled around their bills so that they cannot feed or breathe. Marine animals and fish eat them. Some swim through them, which may squeeze their bodies so they can't breathe. Encourage students to help animals by snipping the rings before they discard them.

## TRICK
# Rhyming Even 6s

Have students say the 6 facts aloud. Challenge them to listen for facts that rhyme: $6 \times 4$ = 24, $6 \times 6 = 36$, and $6 \times 8 = 48$. Guide them to notice that in these three facts, each is 6 times an even number. Also, the product is formed by two numbers that double each other: 2 and 4, 3 and 6, 4 and 8. Have students say these facts aloud in a rhythmic way to emphasize the rhyme and the pattern. The rule of rhyming even 6s can help students isolate these particular facts to make them easier to remember. This rule doesn't hold for $6 \times 2 = 12$ or $6 \times 10 = 60$, but students can use other rules to help recall those facts.

## CONCEPT
# Breakdown!

Help students discover the relationship between the 3s and the 6s. Challenge students to show why, say, $6 \times 6$ is the same as $(2 \times 6) + (2 \times 6) + (2 \times 6)$. Have them write six 6s in a column on their paper. Model how to use brackets to show three groups of two 6s per group. The total of one group of $2 \times 6$ *(12)* is the same as the total of each other group of $2 \times 6$, so $6 \times 6 = 12 + 12 + 12 = 36$. Many students use this technique to find products of 6 as a series of additions of doubles. Some may realize that these sets of products have the same relationship as the products of the 2s and 4s (see page 24). This technique has a solid conceptual foundation students can use to figure out a 6 fact.

$$6 \atop 6 \Big\rangle 12$$
$$\Big\rangle 24$$
$$6 \atop 6 \Big\rangle 12$$

$$6 \atop 6 \Big\rangle 12 \rightarrow \begin{matrix} +12 \\ \hline 36 \end{matrix}$$

## MANIPULATIVES
# Egg Carton Sixes

Obtain an assortment of empty egg cartons. Ask students to give another name for a quantity of 12. *(dozen)* Ask how many things are in a half dozen. *(6)* Encourage students to use the egg cartons to model the 6 facts. Challenge them to think about 6s in relation to dozens by asking questions like these:

⊚ How many 6s can you show with 3 egg cartons? *(6)*

⊚ How many cartons do you need to show 4 x 6? *(2)*

# 7 AS A FACTOR

A calendar is the most common place students encounter groups of 7. Sports fans often find multiples of 7 in football scores. Because many of the 7 facts also come up in other sets of products, there are really just a few that pose problems for most students.

## FACT BOOKLET
## Football 7s

Use the pattern below as a template for an individual fact booklet for the 7s. Discuss why this kind of ball makes sense to use for a booklet about 7s. *(In football, when a team scores a touchdown and the extra point, it earns 7 points. Football scores are often multiples of 7.)* Have students trace and cut out 11 copies of the football shape from white or colored paper. On each one, have them write a 7 fact and its product, from $0 \times 7 = 0$ through $10 \times 7 = 70$. Help them attach the pages in order with yarn, a paper fastener, or staples. Children may customize each page with a symbol, a color, or the logo or name of a different football team to help them more readily recall the facts. Children can use the booklet to study the 7s on their own.

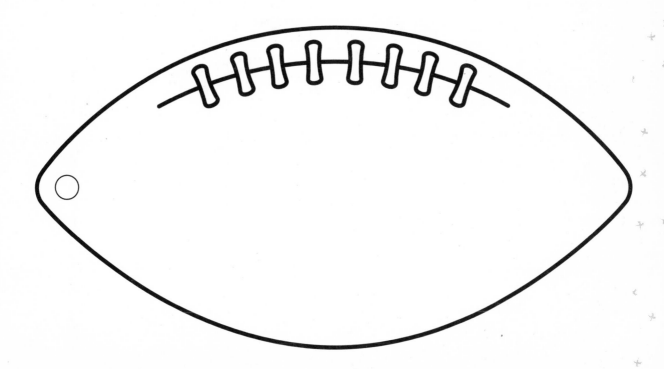

# Calendar 7s

Use old calendars to help students count multiples of 7. Point out that one week has 7 days: Sunday, Monday, Tuesday, Wednesday, Thursday, Friday, and Saturday. Most calendars use an array with some number of rows of 7 to represent the days in a month (or year). Ask students to find the seventh of the current month and identify the day on which it falls. Then ask:

 What is the date one week later? *(the 14th)*

 What date is two weeks from the seventh? *(the 21st)*

 What date is three weeks after the seventh? *(the 28th)*

 What pattern do these dates show? *(the first four multiples of 7)*

 Why doesn't the calendar show a 35? *(No month has that many days.)*

Encourage students to explore the calendar to find other number patterns. For instance, they may notice that the difference between any two dates in the same month that are exactly one week apart is always 7; dates two weeks apart have a difference of 14, and so on. Some students may notice that the difference between numbers along a diagonal that moves from upper left to lower right is always 8 *(1 week plus 1 day)*, and the difference between numbers along a diagonal that moves from upper right to lower left is always 6. *(1 week minus 1 day)*

## August

| Sunday | Monday | Tuesday | Wednesday | Thursday | Friday | Saturday |
|--------|--------|---------|-----------|----------|--------|----------|
|        |        | 1       | 2         | 3        | 4      | 5        |
| 6      | 7      | 8       | 9         | 10       | 11     | 12       |
| 13     | 14     | 15      | 16        | 17       | 18     | 19       |
| 20     | 21     | 22      | 23        | 24       | 25     | 26       |
| 27     | 28     | 29      | 30        | 31       |        |          |

# 8 AS A FACTOR

Octets, octagons, octaves, and octopuses (or is it octopi?!)—groups of 8 abound in music, math, and science.

## FACT BOOKLET
## Octopus 8s

Use the pattern below as a template for an individual fact booklet for the 8s. Discuss why this marine animal is an appropriate figure to use for a booklet about 8s. *(An octopus has 8 tentacles, or arms.)* Have students trace and cut out 11 copies of the octopus shape from white or colored paper. On each octopus, have them write an 8 fact and its product, from $0 \times 8 = 0$ through $10 \times 8 = 80$. Help them attach the pages in order with yarn, a paper fastener, or staples. Children may customize each page with a symbol, a color, or stickers that can help them recall the facts. Children can use the booklet to study the 8s on their own.

# SCIENCE
# Arachnid 8s

Explain to students that although they may think a spider is a kind of insect, a spider is actually an *arachnid*, which is a different kind of animal. Spiders always have eight legs; insects have six legs. Guide students to do research on spiders. Create a bulletin board display of spider facts, pictures, poems, and webs.

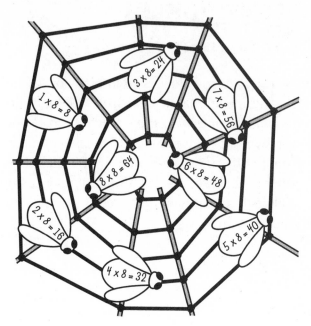

You can follow these steps to preserve a natural spiderweb that students find outdoors. Put a light, even coat of clear enamel spray on both sides of the web. Gently press a piece of oak tag or heavy paper onto the wet web, which should stick to it. Carefully trim the web's anchor lines. Lay the paper down on a flat surface as the web dries. Then you can display it in the classroom.

Or make a large spiderweb from string with sticks as spokelike supports on which to weave. Invite students to write 8 facts on small bug-sized slips of paper, which they can "stick" onto the spiderweb, as if caught there.

# VOCABULARY
# Oct- Words

Tell students that the prefix *oct-*, which comes from the Latin word *octo*, means "eight." Brainstorm with the class to list as many words as students know that begin with *oct-*. Examples include *octagon, octopus, October, octave, octane, octahedron,* and *octuplet*. Challenge students to use a dictionary or other reference materials to find out the "eight-ness" of each word.

# Break Apart Larger Factors

Help students find relationships between the 2s, the 4s, and the 8s. Challenge them to show why, say, $8 \times 6$ has the same value as $(2 \times 6) + (2 \times 6) + (2 \times 6) + (2 \times 6)$. Have students write eight 6s in a row on their paper. Model how to use brackets to combine the eight sixes into four groups of two 6s per group. The total of one group of $2 \times 6$ is 12, so the product is the sum of $12 + 12 + 12 + 12$, or $24 + 24$, or 48. Encourage students to break apart larger factors into smaller facts they know and then combine these products until they've accounted for all groups.

$$8 \times 6 = \quad 6 \; + \; 6 \; + \; 6 \; + \; 6 \; + \; 6 \; + \; 6 \; + \; 6 \; + \; 6$$
$$12 \quad + \quad 12 \quad + \quad 12 \quad + \quad 12$$
$$24 \qquad\qquad + \qquad\qquad 24$$
$$48$$

# 5, 6, 7, 8...

Many students find $7 \times 8$ to be one of the hardest multiplication facts to learn. Use this nifty trick to help them remember this tricky fact.

Write the numerals 5, 6, 7, and 8 on the chalkboard. Leave space between the numerals but do not write commas. Then put a bracket beneath the 5 and 6 to suggest 56, put = between the 6 and 7, and put $\times$ between the 7 and 8. This yields the number sentence $56 = 7 \times 8$. Help students recognize that although they may be accustomed to seeing equations with the "answer" to the right of the =, the quantities on both sides of the = have the same value. Apply the order property of multiplication to show that $8 \times 7$ is also 56.

Help students come up with a mnemonic to help them remember when to use this trick. For example, you might tell students that $8 \times 7$ (or $7 \times 8$) is the hardest multiplication fact in the world. This admittedly unsubstantiated claim will inspire them to make sure they overcome the challenge of learning this hard fact!

# Product Sums

Have students write the multiples of 8 in order in a column: 8, 16, 24, 32, 40, 48, 56, 64, 72, 80. Have them find the digit sum of each multiple and look for a pattern. Students may notice that the digit sums are 8, 7, 6, 5, 4, then 12, 11, 10, 9, and 8. Knowing this pattern may help students verify products they are not sure of.

# 9 AS A FACTOR

The great American pastime—baseball—may be one of the most popular occurrences of 9s for students. The 9 players in a team lineup and the 9 innings in the game provide opportunities to think about groups of 9 in many ways. Because the 9s yield some interesting patterns, most students find ways to learn them quickly.

## FACT BOOKLET
## Baseball Cap 9s

Use the pattern below as a template for an individual fact booklet for the 9s. Discuss why this kind of hat makes sense as a shape to use for a booklet about 9s. *(A baseball team has 9 players in the lineup; a normal game has 9 innings.)* Have students trace and cut out 11 copies of the cap shape from white or colored paper. On each cap, have them write a 9 fact and its product, from $0 \times 9 = 0$ through $10 \times 9 = 90$. Help them attach the pages in order with yarn, a paper fastener, or staples. Children may customize each page with a team name or logo, a symbol, a color, or small stick-on baseballs that can help them recall the facts. Children can use the booklet to study the 9s on their own.

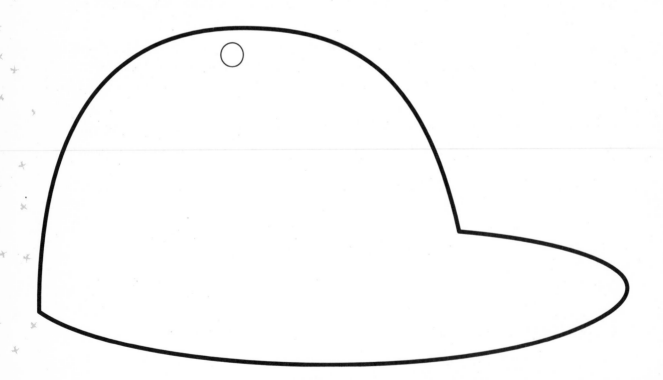

## SPORTS
# Team Spirit

Ask students to name their favorite baseball team. Keep track of the teams on the chalkboard. Invite students to bring in team items, such as a logo cap, pennant, T-shirt, or other souvenir item. Create a bulletin board display for each team. Have students research to put together a lineup of the starting nine players for each team. On the display, include the 9 facts.

Invite students to make up multiplication story problems with a baseball theme. Here are some examples:

- If each player on the Dodgers gets to have 3 strikes, how many strikes are allowed in all? *(3 x 9 = 27)*

- If each player on the Tigers gets 5 free tickets to this Sunday's game, how many free tickets is that in all? *(5 x 9 = 45)*

- The fans at Wrigley Field do "the Wave" 7 times an inning. How many times do they do the Wave during a complete game? *(7 x 9 = 63)*

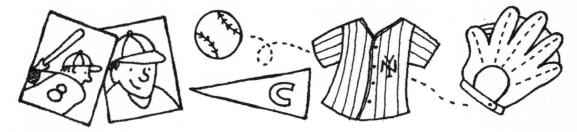

## PATTERN
# Product Digit Sums

List these ten multiples of 9 in a column on the chalkboard: 9, 18, 27, 36, 45, 54, 63, 72, 81, 90. Be sure to align the ones and tens places. Ask students to look for patterns in the numbers. Here are some they may notice:

- The digit sum of each multiple is 9.

- Each subsequent multiple of 9 begins with the next higher counting number.

- Each subsequent multiple of 9 ends with the next lower counting number.

- Each multiple of 9 begins with 1 less than the other factor. That is, 6 x 9 begins with 5, 8 x 9 begins with 7, and so on.

Another pattern some students like is to list multiples of 9 by counting up and back. Here's how: Have them make a two-column place-value chart with tens and ones. Starting at the top of the tens place, they write the counting numbers from 0 to 9, one per row. Then they go to the top of the ones column and write the numbers from 9 to 0, again one per row. When they finish, they will have listed all the multiples of 9 in order, from 9 through 90.

Encourage students to use any of these tricks to help them remember the 9s.

# TRICK
# The 9s Finger Trick

Children are always amazed to find out how useful their fingers can be to help them learn number facts. This trick works only for the 9s, but it works for all products from $0 \times 9$ through $10 \times 9$.

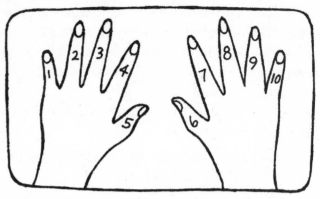

Have students place both hands flat, palms down, fingers outstretched, on a table, desk, or floor. Use a washable marker to number their fingers from 1 to 10, as shown in the illustration.

Have students identify finger number 4, finger number 7, and so on, to be sure they follow the pattern. To find products of nines using the finger trick, students bend down the finger that represents the multiple they want to know. This hidden finger becomes the "divider" between tens and ones. All fingers to the *left* of the hidden finger are tens; all fingers to the *right* of the hidden finger are ones. Children can "read" the product from their hands if they've hidden the right finger. Try this:

Use the finger trick to find $6 \times 9$. Bend down finger number 6, which is the thumb of the right hand. Show students that there are 5 fingers to the left of the hidden finger, representing 10, 20, 30, 40, 50. There are 4 fingers to the right of the hidden finger, representing 1, 2, 3, 4. Therefore, the product of $6 \times 9 = 50 + 4 = 54$.

Have students practice this trick until they can do it without numbering their fingers. They'll love amazing friends and family members. The most dexterous among them can probably find the product faster than a student who uses a calculator! Try it!

# 10 AS A FACTOR

Dimes, decades, bowling pins, our base-10 system of numeration—10s are all around us! Because most students learn to count by 10s in first or second grade, they already know the multiples of 10! Here are a few more ideas to explore.

## FACT BOOKLET
## Tenpin 10s

Use the pattern below as a template for an individual fact booklet for the 10s. Discuss why a bowling pin is a good shape to use for a booklet about 10s. *(Bowling uses 10 pins.)* Have students trace and cut out 11 copies of the bowling pin shape from white or colored paper. On each one, have them write a 10 fact and its product, from $0 \times 10 = 0$ through $10 \times 10 = 100$. Help them attach the pages in order with yarn, a paper fastener, or staples. Children may customize each page with a symbol, a color, or small stickers that can help them recall the facts. Children can use the booklet to study the 10s on their own.

## MANIPULATIVES
# Dime Time

Obtain a quantity of dimes, play or real. Have students use them to count by 10s from 0 (no dimes) to 100 (10 dimes or 1 dollar). Then invite students to play this simple game:

Each player uses a number cube, a spinner, or number cards to generate a random number. The player counts by 10s that many times while taking that number of dimes from the "bank." The first person to accumulate *exactly* ten dimes wins the round.

## PATTERN
# 10 Time

Write all the 10 facts in a column on the board or on an overhead projector. Ask students to describe a pattern in the products. Most will observe that all multiples of 10 end in zero. Also guide them to notice that the leading digit of the product is the same as the factor of 10.

$$0 \times 10 = \mathbf{0}$$
$$1 \times 10 = 1\mathbf{0}$$
$$2 \times 10 = 2\mathbf{0}$$
$$3 \times 10 = 3\mathbf{0}$$
$$4 \times 10 = 4\mathbf{0}$$
$$5 \times 10 = 5\mathbf{0}$$
$$6 \times 10 = 6\mathbf{0}$$
$$7 \times 10 = 7\mathbf{0}$$
$$8 \times 10 = 8\mathbf{0}$$
$$9 \times 10 = 9\mathbf{0}$$
$$10 \times 10 = 10\mathbf{0}$$

Children who understand this rule enjoy extending the pattern to find the products of any number times 10. For example:

$$36 \times 10 = 36\mathbf{0}$$
$$888 \times 10 = 8{,}88\mathbf{0}$$
$$12{,}345 \times 10 = 123{,}45\mathbf{0}$$
$$1 \text{ million} \times 10 = \mathbf{10} \text{ million}$$

Children can also apply this pattern to recognize that products of 10 that do *not* end in zero must be wrong. For example:

$$4 \times 10 \neq 45$$
$$3 \times 10 \neq 31$$
$$16 \times 10 \neq 106$$

## POEM
# Multiply by 10s

Display the following poem on the chalkboard, chart paper, the overhead projector, or duplicate it so that each student can have a copy. Find the rhythm of the poem by reading it aloud. Then divide the class into two groups: for each line of the poem, one group gives the call and the other group gives the response. Practice reading the poem chorally, using the call-and-response technique for the most energetic and enthusiastic presentation.

When students are well acquainted with the poem and how to present it, they can switch sides: the callers become the responders and vice versa. Perform the poem for other groups or videotape it so other classes can view it. You might even borrow some simple rhythm instruments from the music teacher so that musical volunteers can add a lively accompaniment.

| CALL | RESPONSE |
|------|----------|
| How high | *How high* |
| Can you multiply | *Multiply—* |
| By tens | *By tens—* |
| My friends? | *My friends?* |
| All the tens | *Those tens!* |
| With zeros end! | *The end!* |
| Oh the tens | *Tens, tens!* |
| Mighty tens! | *Mighty tens!* |
| | |
| One ten? | *That's ten!* |
| Two tens? | *That's twenty!* |
| Three tens? | *That's thirty!* |
| Four tens? | *That's forty!* |
| Five ten? | *That's fifty!* |
| Six tens? | *That's sixty!* |
| Seven tens? | *That's seventy!* |
| Eight tens? | *That's eighty!* |
| Nine tens? | *That's ninety!* |
| Ten tens? | *That's a hundred!* |
| That's the tens! | *That's the end!* |

# 11 AS A FACTOR

Generally 11s and 12s aren't part of the set of basic multiplication facts. However, students so readily learn some of these facts that it can boost their number sense, mental math skills, and math confidence to investigate patterns among these facts.

## PATTERN
## Easy 11s

Write the first few factors of 11 on the chalkboard: 11, 22, 33, 44... Ask students to describe the pattern they see and continue it through 99. *(Each number has two identical digits; they increase by 11 each time; 55, 66, 77, 88, 99).* Ask students to relate this pattern to the multiplication facts from $0 \times 11$ through $9 \times 11$. Help them determine the next two multiples of 11 to show them what happens to the pattern. Some students may be able to describe how the pattern continues in the subsequent multiples of 11: 110, 121, 132, 143, 154... *(The digits in the tens places increase by one, as do the ones digits, and the ones digit starts with zero; the middle digit is the sum of the outer digits.)*

# 12 AS A FACTOR

## BRAINSTORM
## Daily Dozens

Children encounter groups of 12 in many circumstances in their daily lives: with clocks, the number of hours in a day, and items that come by the dozen, such as eggs. Brainstorm with the class things that often come in dozens. Examples include eggs, pencils, some soft drinks, party invitations, and golf balls. If possible, make a casual field trip to a local hardware or housewares store and let students investigate to find items that are sold by the dozen. Back in the classroom, invite them to create story problems based on the data they gather.

## SCIENCE
## Day by Day

Remind students that one day has 24 hours: we identify 12 hours as A.M. and 12 hours as P.M. This fact helps students remember that $2 \times 12 = 24$.

Some students may have seen or heard of the television news program called *48 Hours*. Help them figure out how many days make 48 hours. *(2)* Break 48 down into groups of 12: $(2 \times 12) + (2 \times 12) = 24 + 24 = 48$.

# Multiplication Applications & More!

## INTERACTIVE BULLETIN BOARD
## Great Grouping

**GOAL:** To reinforce the use of multiplication in everyday life by collecting and displaying objects or pictures of items that come in same-size groups

**YOU NEED:** bulletin board space, paper strips to form columns, old magazines and catalogs, scissors, index cards or self-stick notes, thumbtacks or pushpins

### Here's What to Do

1. Divide bulletin board spaces into as many as ten columns or regions. Label each region with a number from 2 through 10.

2. Divide the class into small groups. Provide each group with some old magazines and catalogs, scissors, and index cards or self-stick notes.

3. Challenge groups to find pictures of things that come in groups of 2, of 3, of 4, and so on. When they find a suitable picture or illustration, they cut it out, tack it in the correct section of the bulletin board, and make an index-card label for it. The label might say something like, "Bicycle wheels come in 2s" or "Feet have 5 toes."

4. Children who have ideas of things that come in same-size groups but cannot find a picture can either draw a picture or list the items on index cards to add to the appropriate section of the board.

Leave this display up for as long as you can. Encourage students to add new pictures or names of items to it whenever they encounter fresh examples.

### To Extend

◉ Use the display as a source of ideas for story problems students can create.

◉ Make multiple copies of some pictures. Post the copies as a set. Have students write a multiplication number sentence that fits the picture. Suppose you post 5 copies of a picture of 2 swans. Students can write $5 \times 2 = 10$.

◉ Revise the display so that it presents a thematic slant, such as science, the community, the grocery store, or sports. Have students display items that come in same-size groups and that also fit the theme.

## INTERACTIVE BULLETIN BOARD
# Hooray for Arrays!

**GOALS:** To illustrate multiplication with rectangular arrays; to model the commutative (order) property of multiplication

**YOU NEED:** bulletin board space, paper strips to form columns, centimeter grid (reproducible page 70), colored markers, scissors, thumbtacks or pushpins

## Here's What to Do

1. Prepare the bulletin board to look like a large, empty multiplication table for the facts from $1 \times 1$ through $10 \times 10$. You can make the size of the grid proportional to the size of the arrays it will hold. In other words, the space for the $8 \times 9$ array should be larger than the space for the $2 \times 3$ array.

2. Label the factors along the top and down the left side of the table.

3. Divide the class into ten groups. Assign each group a number from 1 to 10. Each group is responsible for making a rectangular array for each fact from 1 to 10 for their number. Provide centimeter grids, scissors, and colored markers. Children cut out arrays, label them with a number sentence (i.e., $3 \times 4 = 12$ on a $3 \times 4$ array), and post them along the row where they belong.

4. When the array board is done, each box will hold a labeled grid paper array for each multiplication fact. Leave this display up for as long as you can.

| x | 1 | 2 | 3 | 4 | 5 | |
|---|---|---|---|---|---|---|
| 1 | | | | | | |
| 2 | | | | $4 \times 2 = 8$ | | |
| 3 | | | | | $5 \times 3 = 15$ | |
| 4 | | | $3 \times 4 = 12$ | $4 \times 4 = 16$ | | |
| 5 | | | | $4 \times 5 = 20$ | | |
| 6 | | | $3 \times 6 = 18$ | | $5 \times 6 = 30$ | |

## To Extend

◎ Encourage students to consult the array board to verify products.

◎ Have students find examples that prove the order (commutative) property of multiplication. That is, have them use arrays to prove that $5 \times 3$ has the same number of squares as $3 \times 5$.

◎ Prepare *unlabeled* arrays, one for each space on the array board. Give a random assortment of arrays to each of several groups of students. Challenge them to sort and post the arrays where they go to fill the chart.

# INTERACTIVE BULLETIN BOARD
# Comparing Products

**GOALS:** To practice multiplication facts; to compare products; to use the mathematical symbols for inequality (< and >)

**YOU NEED:** bulletin board space, multiplication fact cards *without products*, large inequality symbols, paper "frames" for the fact cards, thumbtacks or pushpins

## Here's What to Do

1. Set aside bulletin board space large enough to display two multiplication facts as an inequality, such as $3 \times 5 < 4 \times 4$.

2. Post a large inequality symbol (< or >) in the center of the space. Make colored paper "frames" in which students can arrange any two fact cards to form an inequality.

3. Randomly post other multiplication fact cards elsewhere on the bulletin board.

4. Invite a volunteer to come to the board to create a multiplication inequality. The student can select any two facts from the posted facts and arrange them so that the inequality statement is true.

5. Allow students to rearrange the fact cards throughout the day to form other true inequality statements. On subsequent days, use the opposite symbol or post different facts to keep the display fresh and challenging.

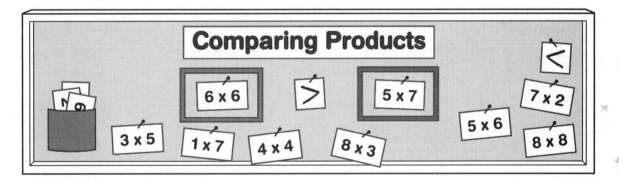

## To Extend

◉ Post three to five facts. Challenge students to make as many possible true inequality statements as they can, given those facts.

◉ Include an equals symbol (=). Challenge students to arrange multiplication fact cards that will work with that symbol, such as $2 \times 8 = 4 \times 4$.

◉ As students learn many of the easier facts, post only the more difficult or troublesome facts, such as $6 \times 8$, $7 \times 7$, $8 \times 7$, $9 \times 6$, or those whose products are close, such as $7 \times 3$, $3 \times 8$, $2 \times 11$, $5 \times 5$, $3 \times 9$, and $4 \times 7$.

# INTERACTIVE BULLETIN BOARD
# Product Sort

**GOALS:** To practice multiplication facts; to sort products in various ways; to make generalizations about multiplication facts

**YOU NEED:** bulletin board space, multiplication fact cards *without products*, paper strips to form regions, paper labels, thumbtacks or pushpins

## Here's What to Do

**1.** Divide the bulletin board into two parts. Label each part with a related but contrasting idea for sorting multiplication facts. Here are some possibilities:

- products greater than 50/less than 50
- even/odd products
- products that end in 0–4/in 5–9
- products with a digit sum of 4 or less/of 5 or more

**2.** Post 15–20 multiplication fact cards in random order at the bottom of the space.

**3.** Invite volunteers to sort the fact cards into the regions where they belong.

**4.** Vary the display by altering the labels or by providing different sets of fact cards for students to sort.

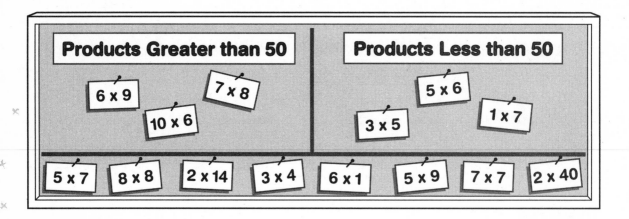

## To Extend

- Form three regions. Label each region with a different unifying idea.
- Label a region with a more advanced idea, such as "products that are divisible by 3" or "products that are square numbers."
- Sort multiplication fact cards that go together in some way, but don't reveal the rule. Challenge students to determine what rule you used. Talk about the responses together.

# INTERACTIVE BULLETIN BOARD
# Clip-On Products

**GOALS:** To provide an interactive way to practice multiplication facts; to reinforce the use of a multiplication table

**YOU NEED:** bulletin board space, large poster board, straightedge, markers, paper clips, razor knife, masking tape, oak tag cut into small squares

## Here's What to Do

1. Divide the poster board into 11 rows and columns for a table of multiplication facts from $0 \times 0$ through $10 \times 10$. Use markers and a straightedge to form grid lines. Do *not* write in any numbers.

2. Using a razor knife, make a small horizontal slit at the top of each box of the grid. Put a paper clip through the slot. Tape the paper clips into place with masking tape across the back of the poster board. (Students will be posting and removing product cards to fill in the table.)

3. Cut out small pieces of oak tag to a size that will fit the boxes of the table. Make two set of factor cards, from 0 to 10. Clip them into place along the top of the table and down the left side.

4. Make product cards for all products that go on the table ($0 \times 0$ through $10 \times 10$). Put them in an envelope or tack them around the outside of the table.

5. Let students slip the product cards where they belong to complete the table. You can start with a completely blank table, or you can leave a particular row or column incomplete if you want to focus on particular facts.

## To Extend

⊚ Challenge groups to fill in the table as fast as they can, or within a particular time limit.

⊚ Post products in the wrong places. Challenge students to rearrange them to make the chart correct.

⊚ For a more difficult task, rearrange the factor cards into random order. This makes it harder for students to fill in the table because products don't appear in their usual place.

## CHART
# Product Strips

**GOAL:** To provide a tool students can use to practice multiplication facts

**YOU NEED:** template (see right), markers

### Here's What to Do

**1.** Copy the template, which shows a 2 × 12 array. Make one copy for each child.

**2.** Distribute the templates. Have students fill in the factors and products for a set of multiples. Here's an example for the sevens:

| X | 0 | 1 | 2 | 3 | 4 | 5 | 6 | 7 | 8 | 9 | 10 |
|---|---|---|---|---|---|---|---|---|---|---|----|
| 7 | 0 | 7 | 14 | 21 | 28 | 35 | 42 | 49 | 56 | 63 | 70 |

**3.** If they want, students can use different colors for the factors and for the products. Or they can highlight especially troublesome products in a certain color, to help them visualize the fact more readily.

### To Extend

◎ Have partners test each other using the product charts they most need to practice.

◎ Use product charts as mini-quizzes on certain facts.

# FAST TIMES

## QUICKIE
# Fact of the Day

Obtain or make a fancy picture frame. Display it in a prominent spot. Mount a banner above the frame that says FACT OF THE DAY. Each day or two, put one multiplication fact inside the picture frame. Pause from time to time during the day to ask students to give the product of that special fact. Surprise them by asking as they line up for gym or before they leave for lunch. Interrupt a reading group by asking them to tell the fact of the day. The unexpected and whimsical nature of this approach helps students remember facts and makes memorizing more entertaining and automatic.

## QUICKIE
# Time for Times

On the 1950s TV game show *You Bet Your Life*, comedian/host Groucho Marx would tell the audience a secret word. If a contestant happened to mention that word during the game, a silly-looking duck would drop down from the ceiling with the word in its bill, and the person would win a special prize.

Try a takeoff on this. Tell students that you've chosen a secret multiplication word for the day (such as *times, product, factor, table, multiply, double, triple,* or *twice*). Get some little prizes, such as stickers, paper prize ribbons, new pencils, or passes to the library. Write the secret word on a card, seal the card in an opaque envelope, and post it in plain sight. The first person who happens to say the secret word—not during math time—wins a prize.

As a variation, if anyone says the secret word, have the class stop whatever it's doing, stand up, and shout out the multiplication fact of the day.

## QUICKIE
# One-Minute Madness

How do you get to Carnegie Hall? Practice, practice, practice!

The same is true for mastering the multiplication facts. The more students practice the basic facts, the more quickly they will memorize them. Set aside a minute each day for an informal speed drill—right before lunch or recess, to start off or wind up a math class, or to end class meeting time.

You can present just two or three facts. You can give the drill orally, chorally, at the board, or independently. You might use product strips (see page 48), or have a race to the board to point to the correct product for a given fact. Vary the technique, but practice consistently. Children enjoy the challenge and they'll love that the task is so short.

# Chart Art

**GOALS:** To identify the many number patterns that appear in a basic 100 chart; to recognize the importance of patterns in mathematics

**YOU NEED:** Hundred Chart (reproducible page 68), colored pencils or crayons

## Here's What to Do

**1.** Duplicate and distribute three copies of reproducible page 68 to each student.

**2.** Post a color key for the multiples of each number, such as:

multiples of 2 = yellow
multiples of 3 = green
multiples of 4 = red
multiples of 5 = blue
multiples of 6 = purple
multiples of 7 = gray
multiples of 8 = orange
multiples of 9 = brown
multiples of 10 = white

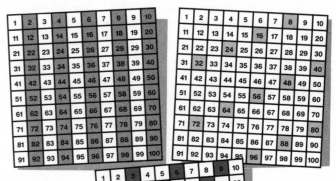

**3.** Help each student select three different number patterns to color, one on each chart. For instance, one student might color all the 2s, the 5s, and the 8s, while another colors all the 4s, the 6s, and the 10s. Guide students to pick at least one set of higher multiples.

**4.** When students finish coloring, regular patterns will emerge. Display the patterns around the classroom. Encourage students to discuss what they see.

## To Extend

◉ Challenge students to identify numbers common to two different patterns. For instance, 14 is shaded on the 2s chart and on the 7s chart. Extend by having students find numbers that are shaded on three or more charts.

◉ Have students try to color two or three different multiples patterns on the same chart. What happens? Why?

# Times Terms

**GOAL:** To provide a puzzle based on multiplication terminology

**YOU NEED:** Times Terms (reproducible page 52)

## Here's What to Do

**1.** Duplicate and distribute reproducible page 52 to individuals or pairs.

**2.** Have students fill in the word that matches the description. Tell them that if they complete the puzzle correctly, the letters in the shaded boxes can be unscrambled to spell another multiplication word.

**3.** You can provide hints in the form of a word key. On the word key, give all the pertinent multiplication words in alphabetical order. Allow students one peek at the word key if they get stuck. The word key would contain these words: *addition, double, factor, multiply, product, same size, times, triple,* and *zero.* The scrambled word is *multiples.*

## To Extend

◎ Challenge students to make up other puzzles that use multiplication words. For instance, they can scramble multiplication words, hold a multiplication word spelling bee, or make up a multiplication word search.

◎ In their math journals, have students write their own definitions or descriptions of or statements that use key multiplication words.

# Times Terms

Figure out the multiplication word that fits each clue. Write it in the boxes. When you finish, copy the letters in the shaded boxes. Unscramble these letters to form another multiplication word.

**1.** Any number multiplied by this number comes out 0. □ ▨ □ □

**2.** Another word for *multiplied by* is _____. □ □ □ □ ▨

**3.** This is one of the numbers you multiply. □ □ □ ▨ □ □

**4.** When you multiply a number by 3, you _____ that number. □ □ □ □ □ ▨ □

**5.** Multiply a number by 2 to get the same answer as adding a _____.
□ □ ▨ □ □ □

**6.** The answer when you multiply is called the _____. ▨ □ □ □ □ □ □

**7.** Its math symbol is ×. □ □ □ □ □ □ ▨ □

**8.** Multiplication is the same as repeated _____. □ □ □ □ □ ▨ □ □

**9.** You can multiply if you have groups that are the _____ _____ (2 words).
□ □ ▨ □  □ □ □ □

**Write the letters from the shaded boxes here.**

**Now unscramble them to make another word.**

□ □ □ □ □ □ □ □ □

**Tell what this word means.** _____

_____

*The Mega-Fun Multiplication Facts Activity Book* Scholastic Professional Books

# GAME
# Multipli-Carton

**GOAL:** To provide mixed practice of multiplication facts

**YOU NEED:** empty egg carton with a top that closes, marker or pen, two beads

## Here's What To Do

1. Number each empty cup in the egg carton. Use numbers from 0 through 11, in order or mixed. If you'd rather not use 11, repeat any other number.

2. Divide the class into groups. Give each group a prepared egg carton and two beads. Children put the beads inside the carton and close the top. The first player shakes the carton, then opens it. He or she gives the product of the two numbers of the cups in which the beads have landed. If both beads are in the same cup, the player multiplies the number by itself, such as $5 \times 5$.

## To Extend

◎ Renumber the cups to include repeats of the most troublesome factors.

◎ Devise a scoring plan. Ideas include keeping a running total of products, or giving different point values to different kinds of products (for example, even products = 2 points, odd products = 3 points, square numbers = 4 points).

# PUZZLE
# Fact Search

**GOAL:** To identify multiplication number sentences

**YOU NEED:** Fact Search (reproducible page 54)

## Here's What to Do

1. Duplicate and distribute reproducible page 54 to individuals or pairs.

2. Tell students that the grid has hidden multiplication number sentences given horizontally, vertically, and diagonally. When students find a number sentence, they draw a ring around it. Number sentences will overlap. *(The only numbers NOT part of a multiplication number sentence are: 5 [row 1], 9 [row 5], 3 [row 6], and 11, 2, and 8 [row 10].)*

## To Extend

◎ Have students make up their own multiplication fact search puzzles.

◎ Make up more advanced fact search puzzles with greater products.

# Fact Search

The puzzle below has many hidden multiplication number sentences. You'll find number sentences going across, up and down, and at an angle. Most number sentences overlap. Only SIX numbers in the whole grid are *not* part of a number sentence. Loop each multiplication number sentence you find. Happy searching!

| 6 | 5 | 0 | 70 | 24 | 1 | 8 | 8 | 64 |
|---|---|---|----|----|---|---|---|----|
| 8 | 0 | 7 | 1 | 6 | 12 | 1 | 7 | 7 |
| 48 | 10 | 0 | 3 | 4 | 7 | 8 | 56 | 6 |
| 90 | 10 | 9 | 3 | 7 | 21 | 42 | 21 | 7 |
| 9 | 100 | 5 | 16 | 28 | 5 | 7 | 35 | 42 |
| 2 | 4 | 8 | 50 | 8 | 3 | 24 | 5 | 3 |
| 20 | 2 | 40 | 10 | 4 | 6 | 6 | 36 | 35 |
| 4 | 6 | 80 | 2 | 32 | 18 | 9 | 18 | 4 |
| 7 | 7 | 49 | 20 | 5 | 4 | 54 | 9 | 6 |
| 11 | 42 | 28 | 2 | 8 | 10 | 36 | 2 | 24 |

*The Mega-Fun Multiplication Facts Activity Book* Scholastic Professional Books

Name _____     Date _____

# Cross-Number Products

Solve this puzzle to practice your multiplication facts.
All answers are numbers.

## Across

**1.** $4 \times 8 =$

**2.** $9 \times 9 =$

**3.** $8 \times 8 =$

**4.** $5 \times 5 =$

**5.** $5 \times 8 =$

**6.** $10 \times 9 =$

**7.** $4 \times 7 =$

**8.** $7 \times 7 =$

**10.** $1 \times 11 =$

**11.** $8 \times 9 =$

**12.** $3 \times 11 =$

**13.** $9 \times 6 =$

**14.** $6 \times 5 =$

**15.** $5 \times 3 =$

**16.** $2 \times 8 =$

**17.** $11 \times 8 =$

**19.** $9 \times 5 =$

**20.** $11 \times 1 =$

**21.** $5 \times 4 =$

**22.** $3 \times 8 =$

**23.** $5 \times 10 =$

**24.** $3 \times 3 =$

## Down

**1.** $7 \times 5 =$

**2.** $8 \times 10 =$

**3.** $10 \times 6 =$

**4.** $3 \times 9 =$

**5.** $6 \times 8 =$

**6.** $11 \times 9 =$

**7.** $3 \times 7 =$

**8.** $7 \times 6 =$

**9.** $9 \times 7 =$

**10.** $7 \times 2 =$

**11.** $7 \times 10 =$

**12.** $5 \times 7 =$

**13.** $8 \times 7 =$

**14.** $4 \times 9 =$

**15.** $6 \times 3 =$

**16.** $3 \times 5 =$

**17.** $9 \times 9 =$

**18.** $10 \times 10 =$

**19.** $4 \times 11 =$

**20.** $5 \times 2 =$

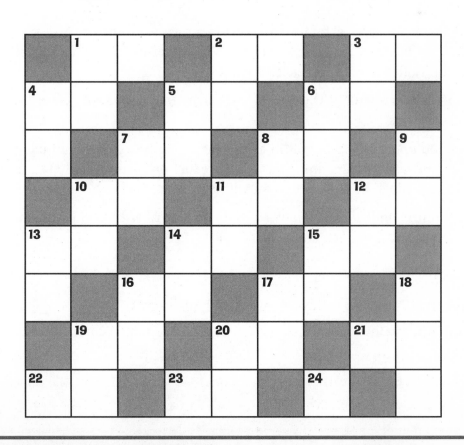

# GAME
# Multipl-O

**GOAL:** To give mixed practice in multiplication facts through a game like Bingo

**YOU NEED:** Multipl-O cards (see below), markers (dried beans, counters, centimeter cubes), multiplication fact cards

## Here's What to Do

**1.** Prepare an assortment of Multipl-O cards. Each card should have a random set of products in a 5 × 5 grid, like a Bingo card. Mark the center space *Free*. Here are two sample cards:

| 18 | 64 | 12 | 25 | 4 |
|----|----|----|----|----|
| 9 | 27 | 24 | 81 | 63 |
| 30 | 32 | FREE | 35 | 16 |
| 27 | 40 | 48 | 56 | 10 |
| 14 | 72 | 45 | 20 | 49 |

| 2 | 24 | 16 | 36 | 8 |
|----|----|----|----|----|
| 40 | 32 | 6 | 54 | 12 |
| 28 | 10 | FREE | 21 | 64 |
| 18 | 15 | 35 | 4 | 56 |
| 25 | 63 | 72 | 30 | 49 |

**2.** The object of the game is to get 5 markers in a row horizontally, vertically, or diagonally, or to fill all 4 corners. To get a space, the player matches the product in a box with a multiplication fact the caller gives.

**3.** Give each player a Multipl-O card and some markers. Players may cover the *Free* space as a bonus.

**4.** Put the multiplication fact cards in a box. The caller draws a card at random, reads the fact, and gives players time to find the product on their Multipl-O cards. If a player has the product, he or she covers it with a marker.

**5.** Play continues until someone has "Multipl-O!" The caller then checks that the products the player covered match the facts called.

## To Extend

⊙ Have students make up their own sets of Multipl-O cards.

⊙ Vary the rules so that the winner is the first player to totally cover his or her card.

# GAME
# Product War

**GOAL:** To provide mixed multiplication fact practice by playing a game like the card game War.

**YOU NEED:** multiplication fact cards

## Here's What to Do

1. Ask a volunteer to tell the rules of the classic card game War. Explain that in Product War, two players turn over cards with multiplication facts. Whichever player's fact has the higher product wins both cards.

2. If players turn over two facts that have the *same* product, such as $4 \times 2$ and $2 \times 4$, or $3 \times 4$ and $2 \times 6$, this is "war." The players turn over three more cards and compare the third one. Whichever player's card has the higher product wins *all* the cards used in that turn.

3. Play continues until one player has captured all the cards, or until time runs out. The player with more cards wins.

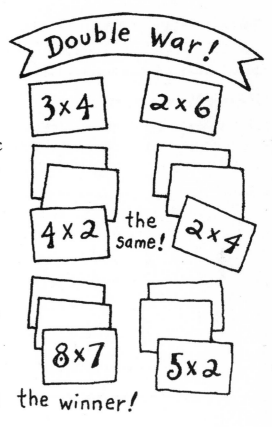

## To Extend

Have students play in groups of three or four to provide more products to compare.

# Multiplication Concentration

**GOALS:** To provide practice with mixed multiplication facts by playing a game like the classic Concentration; to improve visual memory

**YOU NEED:** index cards (or construction paper cut into card-sized pieces)

## Here's What to Do

1. Divide the class into pairs. Ask a volunteer to explain the rules of the old card game Concentration. Explain that Multiplication Concentration is played the same way, but players must match a multiplication fact with its product.

2. Help each pair make a set of 18 multiplication fact cards and 18 product cards. You can list the facts students should use, or let them choose the facts themselves. Each fact card must have a related product card, like this:

### Fact Card:        Product Card:

| **6 x 7** | **42** |
|:---:|:---:|

3. When partners finish making their deck, they shuffle all cards together. One player deals all cards out facedown in a 6 × 6 array.

4. Players go in turn. Each player turns over two cards. If the cards match—that is, if a fact card matches a product card—the player removes both cards and goes again. If the cards do not match, the player places them facedown in their original positions.

5. Play continues until all cards have been paired and taken. The player with more cards wins.

## To Extend

◉ Vary the number of cards per game.

◉ Make cards for facts with the same products. For example, make a 2 × 6 and a 3 × 4, and two 12s. Allow matches of product cards or fact cards.

# Fact Fill-In

**GOAL:** To provide practice with basic multiplication facts in a game setting

**YOU NEED:** Multiplication Grids (reproducible pages 64 and 65)

## Here's What to Do

1. Duplicate reproducible page 64 onto card stock. Form individual playing tiles by cutting apart the products. Discard the factors.

2. Divide the class into groups of two to four players. Each group needs one set of tiles and a copy of reproducible page 65 to use as a playing board.

3. Tell players that the object of the game is to place product tiles on the multiplication table where they belong. Each player picks 9 tiles at random from the complete set. The first player to use up all his or her tiles wins.

4. Here's how to move: The first player puts any product tile in its place on the blank multiplication table. That is, a 16 would go in the box where the factors 2 and 8 meet or where the factors 4 and 4 meet. The next player may place one of his or her tiles in any box that horizontally, vertically, or diagonally touches a tile already in play. For example, if the first player puts the 16 where the factors of 4 meet, the next player may place a 9, 12, 15, 20, or 25, because all of those products touch the 16. As more tiles are added to the table, more available spaces open up.

5. If a player has no tile that fits the available spaces on the table, that player draws a new tile from the pile until he or she has a playable product.

6. If a player places a tile incorrectly, he or she must remove the tile and draw a penalty tile. All players work together to judge the correctness of one another's moves.

## To Extend

◎ Make four blank tiles, as in Scrabble™. A player who draws a blank tile may place it anywhere.

◎ Encourage players to create variations on the basic rules. For instance, players may agree that no player draws more than three tiles per turn, or that a player may place *all* tiles that work on any given turn.

## GAME
# Multiplication Jeopardy

**GOAL:** To work backward to identify possible factors for a given product

**YOU NEED:** multiplication product cards (see below)

### Here's What to Do

1. Discuss the format of the TV game show *Jeopardy,* in which players formulate questions to match given facts.

2. Divide the class into groups of three to six players. Two or three students are players; the others act as questioners and judges.

3. Cut apart the products from a completed multiplication table. To play, the questioner shows a product at random. Players raise their hands when they know a pair of factors that forms that product. The questioner calls on the player who responds first. If the given factors are correct, the player earns 1 point. If the factors do *not* fit the product, the player loses 1 point. In that case, another player may try to give the factors to earn the point.

4. Play continues until one team reaches a score of 15, or until time runs out. The player or team with the most points wins.

### To Extend

Use a varied point system: harder products earn 2 points, easier ones earn 1 point. Allow players or teams to ask for the level of difficulty they'd like.

## GAME
# Product Add-On

**GOAL:** To accumulate a running total that is the sum of products.

**YOU NEED:** 0–10 number cards (reproducible page 67), paper and pencil, calculators (optional)

### Here's What to Do

1. Divide the class into pairs or small groups. Give each group two sets of 0–10 number cards. These become the factors players multiply.

2. To play, each student randomly draws two number cards and finds their product. The product is that player's score for the turn. On subsequent turns, players add new products to the previous ones to keep a running total. The first player to reach or exceed 300 points wins.

### To Extend

◉ Use number cubes or spinners to generate factors.

◉ Use calculators to keep running totals but *not* to find the products.

# Multiplication Stories and Strips

**GOAL:** To create realistic stories or comic strips that involve multiplication

**YOU NEED:** writing paper or word processors, pictures or illustrations, drawing supplies

## Here's What to Do

**1.** Invite students to think of story situations that involve multiplication—the more creative, the better! For instance, students might imagine the number of eyeballs at an alien birthday party, the number of footprints in the snow made by a group of hungry deer, the number of hiccups at a picnic, and so on. Prewriting suggestions include displaying interesting pictures, sharing funny cartoons that involve multiple groups, and reading multiplication stories, such as *One Hundred Hungry Ants* by Elinor J. Pinczes.

**2.** Have each student or pair write a story or other piece of creative writing based on a multiplication fact and an idea they want to explore. Children can write a narrative story, a poem, a skit with dialogue, or a comic strip. Have students create illustrations that fit the mode of writing they select.

**3.** Apply the steps of the writing process to help students write, revise, edit, and present their multiplication stories.

## To Extend

◉ Have a publishing party to celebrate the completion of the multiplication stories and comic strips.

◉ Create an anthology of multiplication stories, poems, comics, and other writings. Display it in the school library, or distribute it to other classes.

◉ Post creative multiplication stories or comics on the Internet.

# SIMULATION
# X-Mart

**GOAL:** To simulate shopping where buyers purchase multiple quantities

**YOU NEED:** small items (or pictures of them), X-Mart Order Forms (reproducible page 63), calculators

## Here's What to Do

1. In your classroom, set up an imaginary store called X-Mart: the X stands for multiplication. "Stock" the store with items priced in 1-digit numbers, such as $1, $4, or $9. You can display sample items, pictures, or descriptions of them.

2. Some students serve as clerks; others are shoppers. Give each store clerk copies of reproducible page 63 to fill out when shoppers decide what to buy.

3. Shoppers get an imaginary $100 to spend in any way they want. All prices include sales tax.

4. Shoppers observe these rules for shopping at X-Mart:
   - They must purchase at least 2, but no more than 10, of any item.
   - They must order at least three different kinds of items.
   - Every purchase requires a completed order form.
   - The total purchase must come as close to $100 as possible without going over.

5. Allow clerks to use calculators as cash registers to total each order.

## To Extend

- Use play money so students can act out the transactions. In this case, set prices between 1¢ and 10¢, and give shoppers $1 to spend.
- Vary the kinds of items in the store, the prices, or the shopping rules.

Name _____  Date_____

# X-Mart Order Form

| HOW MANY? | ITEM | PRICE FOR 1 | TOTAL |
|---|---|---|---|
|  |  |  |  |
|  |  |  |  |
|  |  |  |  |
|  |  |  |  |
|  |  |  |  |
|  |  |  |  |
|  |  |  |  |
|  |  |  |  |
|  |  |  |  |
|  |  |  |  |
|  |  |  |  |
|  |  |  |  |
|  | ← TOTAL ITEMS        GRAND TOTAL COST → |  |  |

Name _____  Date _____

# Multiplication Grid for Factors 0-10 with Products

| ×  | 0 | 1  | 2  | 3  | 4  | 5  | 6  | 7  | 8  | 9  | 10  |
|----|---|----|----|----|----|----|----|----|----|----|-----|
| 0  | 0 | 0  | 0  | 0  | 0  | 0  | 0  | 0  | 0  | 0  | 0   |
| 1  | 0 | 1  | 2  | 3  | 4  | 5  | 6  | 7  | 8  | 9  | 10  |
| 2  | 0 | 2  | 4  | 6  | 8  | 10 | 12 | 14 | 16 | 18 | 20  |
| 3  | 0 | 3  | 6  | 9  | 12 | 15 | 18 | 21 | 24 | 27 | 30  |
| 4  | 0 | 4  | 8  | 12 | 16 | 20 | 24 | 28 | 32 | 36 | 40  |
| 5  | 0 | 5  | 10 | 15 | 20 | 25 | 30 | 35 | 40 | 45 | 50  |
| 6  | 0 | 6  | 12 | 18 | 24 | 30 | 36 | 42 | 48 | 54 | 60  |
| 7  | 0 | 7  | 14 | 21 | 28 | 35 | 42 | 49 | 56 | 63 | 70  |
| 8  | 0 | 8  | 16 | 24 | 32 | 40 | 48 | 56 | 64 | 72 | 80  |
| 9  | 0 | 9  | 18 | 27 | 36 | 45 | 54 | 63 | 72 | 81 | 90  |
| 10 | 0 | 10 | 20 | 30 | 40 | 50 | 60 | 70 | 80 | 90 | 100 |

*The Mega-Fun Multiplication Facts Activity Book* Scholastic Professional Books

Name _____     Date _____

# Multiplication Grid
## for Factors 0-10

| ×  | 0 | 1 | 2 | 3 | 4 | 5 | 6 | 7 | 8 | 9 | 10 |
|----|---|---|---|---|---|---|---|---|---|---|----|
| 0  |   |   |   |   |   |   |   |   |   |   |    |
| 1  |   |   |   |   |   |   |   |   |   |   |    |
| 2  |   |   |   |   |   |   |   |   |   |   |    |
| 3  |   |   |   |   |   |   |   |   |   |   |    |
| 4  |   |   |   |   |   |   |   |   |   |   |    |
| 5  |   |   |   |   |   |   |   |   |   |   |    |
| 6  |   |   |   |   |   |   |   |   |   |   |    |
| 7  |   |   |   |   |   |   |   |   |   |   |    |
| 8  |   |   |   |   |   |   |   |   |   |   |    |
| 9  |   |   |   |   |   |   |   |   |   |   |    |
| 10 |   |   |   |   |   |   |   |   |   |   |    |

Name _____  Date _____

# Multiplication Grid

| × | | | | | | | | | | | |
|---|---|---|---|---|---|---|---|---|---|---|---|
| | | | | | | | | | | | |
| | | | | | | | | | | | |
| | | | | | | | | | | | |
| | | | | | | | | | | | |
| | | | | | | | | | | | |
| | | | | | | | | | | | |
| | | | | | | | | | | | |
| | | | | | | | | | | | |
| | | | | | | | | | | | |
| | | | | | | | | | | | |
| | | | | | | | | | | | |

*The Mega-Fun Multiplication Facts Activity Book* Scholastic Professional Books

# Number Cards

| | | |
|---|---|---|
| 0 | 1 | 2 |
| 3 | 4 | 5 |
| 6 | 7 | 8 |
| 9 | 10 | x |

Name _____     Date _____

# Hundred Chart

| 1 | 2 | 3 | 4 | 5 | 6 | 7 | 8 | 9 | 10 |
|---|---|---|---|---|---|---|---|---|----|
| 11 | 12 | 13 | 14 | 15 | 16 | 17 | 18 | 19 | 20 |
| 21 | 22 | 23 | 24 | 25 | 26 | 27 | 28 | 29 | 30 |
| 31 | 32 | 33 | 34 | 35 | 36 | 37 | 38 | 39 | 40 |
| 41 | 42 | 43 | 44 | 45 | 46 | 47 | 48 | 49 | 50 |
| 51 | 52 | 53 | 54 | 55 | 56 | 57 | 58 | 59 | 60 |
| 61 | 62 | 63 | 64 | 65 | 66 | 67 | 68 | 69 | 70 |
| 71 | 72 | 73 | 74 | 75 | 76 | 77 | 78 | 79 | 80 |
| 81 | 82 | 83 | 84 | 85 | 86 | 87 | 88 | 89 | 90 |
| 91 | 92 | 93 | 94 | 95 | 96 | 97 | 98 | 99 | 100 |

*The Mega-Fun Multiplication Facts Activity Book* Scholastic Professional Books

Name _____  Date _____

# 1/2-inch Grid

Name _____    Date _____

# Centimeter Grid

Name _____ Date _____

# Self-Assessment Log

**1.** In multiplication, I'm especially good at _____

_____

_____

**2.** In multiplication, I need more work on _____

_____

_____

**3.** Before this year, I didn't know _____

_____

_____

**4.** The easiest facts for me are _____

_____

_____

**5.** The hardest facts for me are _____

_____

_____

**6.** A good way for me to learn facts is to _____

_____

_____

**7.** A multiplication game I like is _____

_____

_____

**8.** Next year, I hope to learn _____

_____

_____

# LITERATURE LIST
# Books That Feature Multiplication

Children's literature, including picture books, can provide many opportunities for mathematical thinking and communicating. You can use any of these books to explore multiplication.

*Bunches and Bunches of Bunnies* by Louise Mathews

*Counting by Kangaroos: A Multiplication Concept Book* by Joy N. Hulme

*Ella Vanilla's Multiplication Secrets: Building Math Memory, Rhythm, and Rhyme* by Rosella Wallace

*How Many Feet in the Bed?* by Diane Johnston Hamm

*Lucy and Tom's 1, 2, 3* by Shirley Hughes

*Mice Twice* by Joseph Low

*Noah's Ark Song* by June Epstein

*Number Families* by Jane Srivastava

*One Hundred Hungry Ants* by Elinor J. Pinczes

*Sea Squares* by Joy N. Hulme

*Shoes in Twos* by Rosemary Irons and Calvin Irons

*Trucks You Can Count On* by Doug Magee

*Two Hundred Rabbits* by L. Anderson

*2 x 2 = Boo! A Set of Spooky Multiplication Stories* by Loreen Leedy

*Two Ways to Count to Ten* retold by Ruby Dee

*What Comes in 2's, 3's, and 4's?* by Suzanne Aker